SLIM GOODBODY ™

What Can Go Wrong and How to Be Strong

by John Burstein

**Designed by
J. Paul Kirouac
Photographed by
Russell Dian
Illustrated by
Craigwood Phillips.
A Good Thing, Inc.**

McGraw-Hill Book Company

New York/St. Louis/San Francisco
Auckland/Bogotá/Düsseldorf
Johannesburg/London/Madrid
Mexico/Montreal/New Delhi
Panama/Paris/São Paulo
Singapore/Sydney/Tokyo/Toronto

**Dedicated to my mother,
who gets better all the time,
and my father,
who taught me how to be strong.**

**Special thanks for technical advice to Stanley Freeman D.D.S.
Assistant Professor of Dentistry, Columbia University and
Victor LaCerva M.D. Pediatrician and child at heart.**

My deep appreciation to John Mernit for all his help.

Love to June and Babycakes.

Costume © 1974 by John Burstein.
Costume constructed at Ray Diffen Stage Clothes, Inc., New York, N.Y.

123456789   RABP   78321098

Library of Congress Cataloging in Publication Data

Burstein, John.
    Slim Goodbody, what can go wrong and how to be strong.

    SUMMARY: Answers common questions about health and explains many of the human
body's mysteries including its ability to heal itself.
    1. Diseases — Juvenile literature.   2. Health — Juvenile literature.
[1. Health.   2. Body, Human.   3. Diseases]   I. Kirouac, J. Paul.
II. Title.
R130.5.B87   616   78-18434
ISBN 0-07-009242-7

A Guide to What's Inside

Even though your body is remarkably strong,
now and then there's something that will probably go wrong.

A fall, a scratch,
a chill you catch.
An ache, a pain,
a break or sprain,
cuts and lumps,
the flu and mumps...

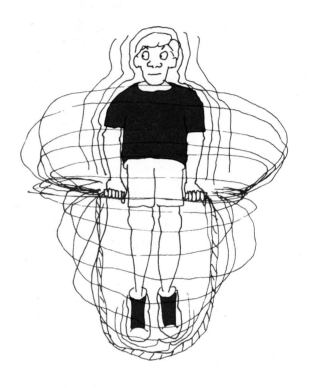

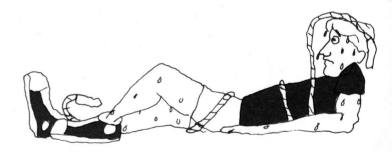

this book you're reading will explore,
these problems and a whole lot more.

If you happen to feel sickly
and in need of some repair,
just give your body very quickly
a great big dose of love and care.
With your inner healing power
and the help of medicine,
you'll get better hour by hour
till you're feeling well again.

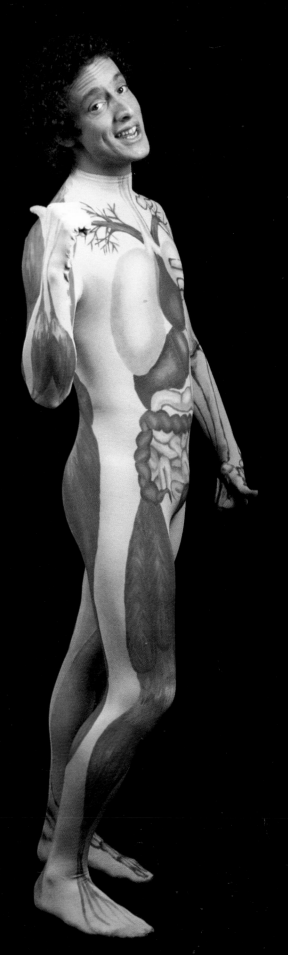

Does your mouth taste funny?
Does your nose get runny?
Do you act a little grumpy?
Do your nerves feel jumpy?
Do you feel real tired?
Do you get perspired?
Are you feeling sad and weepy?
Or just a wee bit creepy?
Is your stomach sort of churning?
Does your skin feel hot and burning?
Or do you feel a shiver?
Do your muscles kind of quiver?
Does your head feel achy?
Are your knees a little shaky?
Would you say you're feeling weak?
Is your throat sore when you speak?

Well my friend, if a few of the above are true for you, then you're probably coming down with...

...a cold

Colds can begin in lots of different ways. You may not even realize you're coming down with one. Very often you'll only get a slight feeling that something is wrong. Try to notice the first warning signal you get, the very first uneasy feeling that lets you know a cold is starting.

The sooner you know you're sick, the sooner you can do something about it.

**I've asked many doctors,
and I've been told,
"There is no sure cure for the common cold."
But most agree
on what is best:
"Drink plenty of fluids, and get lots of rest."**

If you want to stay healthy and help prevent some colds before they start, make sure to take care of yourself *all the time.* This means:

1 Eating wholesome foods in a well-balanced diet.
2 Getting a good night's sleep (eight to ten hours).
3 Wearing clothes that are right for the season.
4 Avoiding drafts and sudden temperature changes.

If you do get a cold, stay in bed while you have a fever, get plenty of rest, and drink a lot more fluids than you usually do. It's a good idea to drink a full glass of something you like (fruit juice, water, herb tea) once every two hours. Maybe your mom or dad will fix you some chicken soup or broth to help you feel better. With proper care your body can heal itself in about a week's time.

It's amazing to realize that we still don't know for sure what causes a cold, but most doctors believe viruses are to blame.
A virus is a tiny germ that can only be seen with a special microscope. Viruses use the materials in the cells of your body in order to multiply.

Did you know that colds are most often spread by sneezing and coughing? You can protect your family and friends by using tissues to catch the cold germs before they escape into the air where others can breathe them. When you blow your nose, do it gently. Keep your mouth open so you don't force cold germs into your ears.

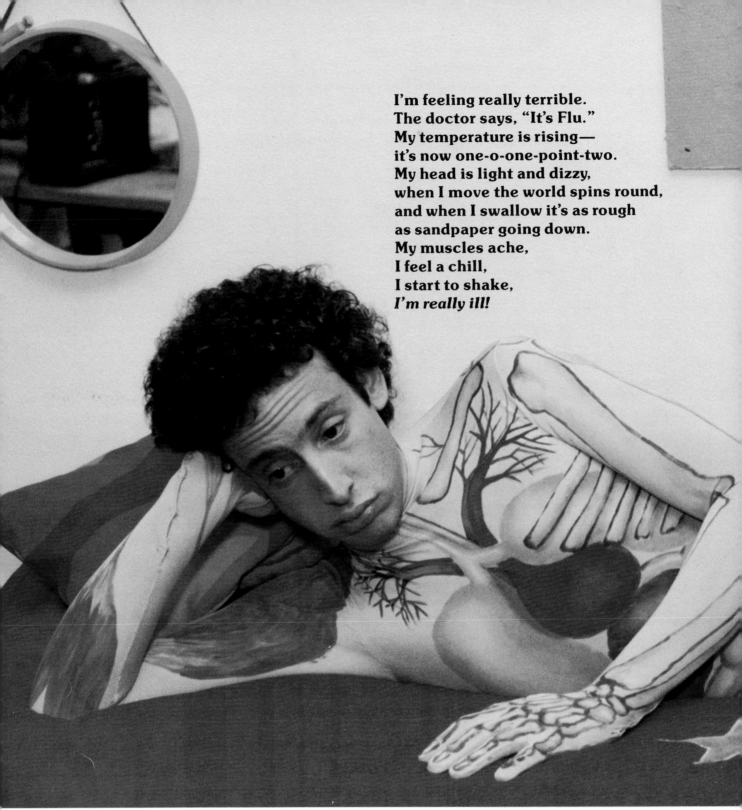

I'm feeling really terrible.
The doctor says, "It's Flu."
My temperature is rising—
it's now one-o-one-point-two.
My head is light and dizzy,
when I move the world spins round,
and when I swallow it's as rough
as sandpaper going down.
My muscles ache,
I feel a chill,
I start to shake,
I'm really ill!

InFLUenza comes on quicker, lasts longer, and is more serious than a cold; it also is far more *contagious.* *

*A disease is contagious if it spreads through direct or indirect contact with a sick person. Direct contagion occurs when you drink from a sick person's glass, or kiss someone who's sick. Indirect contagion happens when you breathe the air into which a sick person has sneezed.

I'm tired of temperature,
tissues, and tea,
talking on telephones,
watching TV.
I've written to relatives,
rested, and read.
It really is dreary
remaining in bed.

It's important to take good care of your body when you get the flu.
Even though staying in bed can be boring, take your time getting
better. With help and advice from your doctor, and tender loving
care from your mom and dad, you'll soon be well again.

Germ

A Body Defense Chemical

A fever is your body's way of telling you "I'm not O.K."

When your temperature rises above normal (98 – 99 degrees), it usually means that your body is fighting some disease. You can think of a fever as the heat from the battle between harmful germs and your body's defense system.

When your body gets warm and turns up the heat, it's forcing a swarm of germs to retreat.

A SWARM OF GERMS

It may sound strange, but a fever can often help your body heal itself. It does this in two important ways:

1. The extra body heat destroys some viruses.
2. Fever speeds up the production of certain chemicals in your body that fight disease.

Of course, not all fevers are helpful. If they are too high or last too long, they can be harmful. Ask your doctor how to bring them down. Aspirin and lukewarm sponge baths usually help.

If you think your temperature must be taken only by grown-ups, then you are mistaken. These next four steps will lead you to be a meter-reader easily.

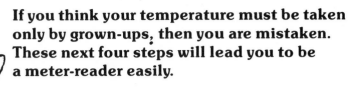

1 **Shake it but don't break it.**
The mercury in the thermometer you use to measure your fever goes up with temperature. But it needs to be shaken down before you use it. Hold the thermometer like this. Make sure your hand isn't near anything. Then, give your wrist a few quick flicks.

1.

2 **Place it carefully under your tongue; remove it when three minutes are done.**
Keep your lips closed to hold the thermometer in place. Don't bite it.

2.

3 **Turn it slowly until you see the very thin line of mercury.**
Make sure you hold the thermometer under a strong light.

3.

4 **Your temperature is normal if the mercury line ends somewhere between 98 and 99.**
The numbers (and the short line underneath) measure degrees of body heat. Anything above 99 degrees means you have a fever.

4.

**There are childhood diseases
I've not mentioned yet,
and at least two or three
you are likely to get.**

Chickenpox

What happens: A rash appears, beginning with a few rose-colored spots on your chest and back. The spots spread over your body, turn into blisters and then dry up and form scabs. The blisters come in a series of breakouts, not all at once.
THEY ITCH AND ITCH AND ITCH!

What you can do: Try not to scratch the blisters. Calamine lotion helps ease the itchiness. Keep your body clean, especially your hands.

Mumps

What happens: There is a swelling around your ears and jaw, first on one side of your face, then on the other. This can make chewing and swallowing very painful.

What you can do: Try to eat soft foods that are easy to swallow.

Whooping Cough

What happens: It starts as an ordinary chest cold with a cough. As a week passes the coughing spells become longer and longer. You may cough eight or nine times in a row without getting a chance to catch your breath. Once the coughing spell stops, you gulp the air in so quickly it sounds like a whoop.

What you can do: Instead of eating three big meals, eat several small ones throughout the day. Make sure there is fresh air in your room.

Measles

What happens:

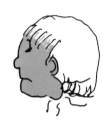

It starts like a cold with fever, sneezing, and coughing. Your eyes become red, puffy, and sensitive to light. You run a high fever, and reddish-brown spots appear, first behind your ears and on your forehead. Soon your whole body is covered with a blotchy, splotchy red rash.

What you can do: Rest in a darkened room so your eyes don't hurt.

German Measles

What happens:

The first thing you may notice is a rash of rose-pink spots (not reddish-brown like measles) that spread from your face to the rest of your body. Your glands* will become swollen behind and below your ears.

What you can do: As always get plenty of rest.

Scarlet Fever

What happens:

Scarlet fever comes on very quickly with high fever, a sore throat, and vomiting. The next day, a rash of red spots starts to spread all over your body—except around your mouth. Your tongue gets swollen and turns bright red.

What you can do: You should make sure to keep your skin clean. Get medicine from your doctor.

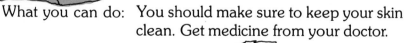
Soap

Strep Throat

What happens: A headache, a fever, and a very sore throat.

What you can do: Keep your skin clean. Get plenty of rest, and drink fluids. Get medicine from your doctor.

*glands, see page 45

There are certain kinds of treatment that should remain the same for every single sickness, no matter what its name.

1 Tell your mother, father, or a friendly adult that you are not feeling well.
2 Speak to a doctor and get his or her advice.
3 Stay in bed while you have a fever.
4 Drink fluids that are good for you (herb tea, juice).
5 Keep away from people until you know your disease is no longer "catching." (Of course, this doesn't mean the people who are caring for you.)
6 As you feel better, get out of bed and do some mild exercising like walking and stretching.

16

DOCTORS' AMMUNITION

**Here's a selection
of pills and injections
that help give protection
from ills and infection.**

Sometimes your inner defenses need some outside help. Then your doctor gives you medicine. You can think of this medicine as ammunition in the battle your body fights against disease.

Some common medicines are:

Aspirin — 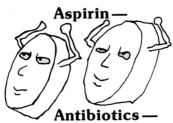 the drug that is most commonly used to relieve fever and mild pain. The most important ingredient originally came from the bark of willow trees, although it now can be produced in laboratories.

Antibiotics — medicine that kills bacteria,* or stops them from multiplying, until your body's natural defenses can take over. Penicillin is an antibiotic which comes from bread mold.

Antihistamines — drugs that sometimes help treat allergic reactions and dry up runny noses.

Anesthetics — drugs that stop you from feeling pain in certain areas.

Remember, drugs can be *very* dangerous, even poisonous. You should only take them when your mother, father, or doctor gives them to you.

Immunization — can help your body resist certain diseases. Children generally get immunized against polio, diptheria, whooping cough (pertussis), tetanus, measles, mumps and German measles (rubella).

*bacteria—tiny one-celled organisms (larger than viruses), which can live and multiply in many different places, including the human body. Some bacteria are harmless, some are helpful, and some cause such diseases as strep throat and whooping cough.

It isn't easy to break a bone,
because they're strong and hard.
But accidents will happen
even in your own backyard.

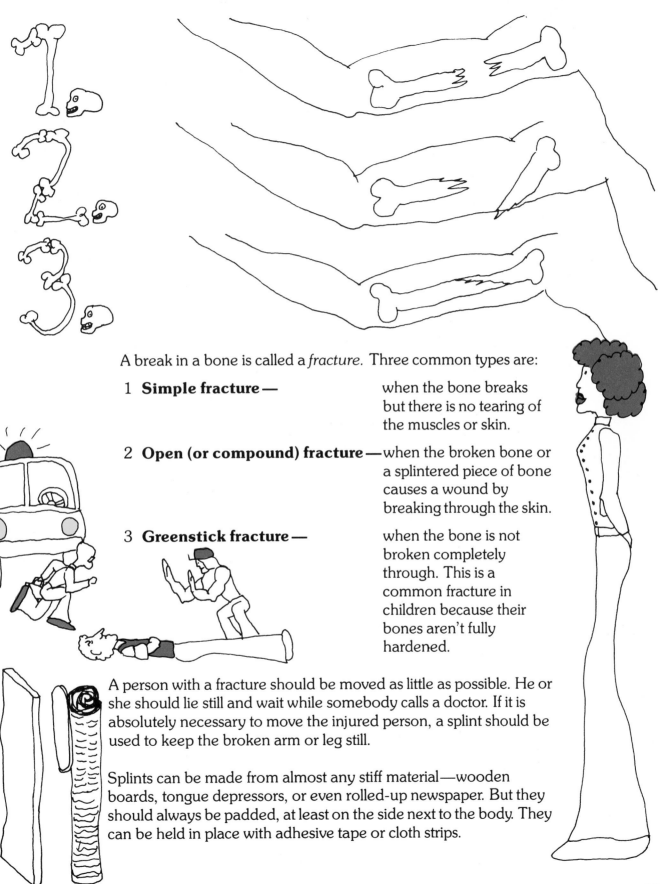

A break in a bone is called a *fracture.* Three common types are:

1 **Simple fracture—** when the bone breaks but there is no tearing of the muscles or skin.

2 **Open (or compound) fracture—** when the broken bone or a splintered piece of bone causes a wound by breaking through the skin.

3 **Greenstick fracture—** when the bone is not broken completely through. This is a common fracture in children because their bones aren't fully hardened.

A person with a fracture should be moved as little as possible. He or she should lie still and wait while somebody calls a doctor. If it is absolutely necessary to move the injured person, a splint should be used to keep the broken arm or leg still.

Splints can be made from almost any stiff material—wooden boards, tongue depressors, or even rolled-up newspaper. But they should always be padded, at least on the side next to the body. They can be held in place with adhesive tape or cloth strips.

Your bones are amazing—
though broken in two,
they'll grow back together
and mend good as new.

Of course you need some help from your doctor. First an X-ray is taken to see exactly what is wrong and what needs to be done. Then the bones are set—lined up straight—so they can grow back together evenly. To make sure they stay that way, your doctor makes a plaster cast. This keeps the person from moving the injured part long enough for the fracture to heal completely. Meanwhile, your body has already begun repairing the damage. Here's how:

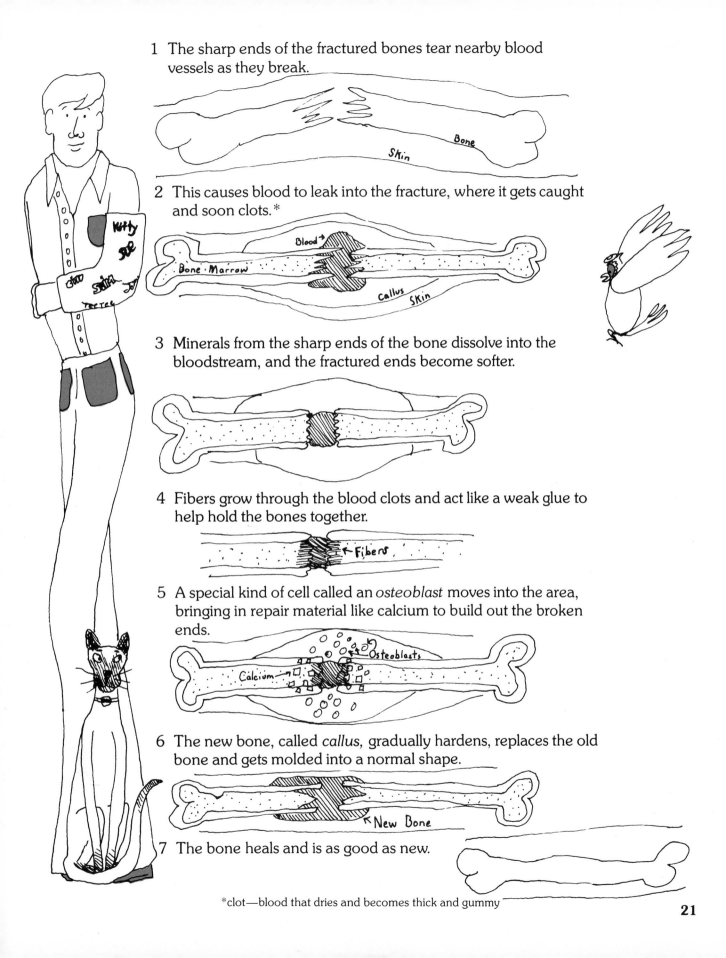

1 The sharp ends of the fractured bones tear nearby blood vessels as they break.

2 This causes blood to leak into the fracture, where it gets caught and soon clots. *

3 Minerals from the sharp ends of the bone dissolve into the bloodstream, and the fractured ends become softer.

4 Fibers grow through the blood clots and act like a weak glue to help hold the bones together.

5 A special kind of cell called an *osteoblast* moves into the area, bringing in repair material like calcium to build out the broken ends.

6 The new bone, called *callus,* gradually hardens, replaces the old bone and gets molded into a normal shape.

7 The bone heals and is as good as new.

*clot—blood that dries and becomes thick and gummy

You can sprain your ankle or sprain your wrist
if you accidentally give it too hard a twist.

You can do it when you slip,
you can do it when you trip,
you can do it when you're practicing
a backward flip.
You can do it when you fall,
you can do it in the hall,
you can do it sliding into first
while playing baseball.

Male Nurse

Your bones are held together at the joints by tough bands of fibers called *ligaments*. You get a sprain when these ligaments are stretched so much that they tear.

Ligaments
Bone
Tendon
Muscle

Sometimes there is a lot of damage, sometimes just a little, but as a general rule: all sprains should be checked out by a doctor or nurse.

For some strange reason, I don't know why,
when I get hurt, it helps to cry.
And I have found when I complain,
it sort of helps relieve the pain.
Now that you know,
here I go—
I *hate* the sprain I got today.
I wish the pain would go away.
My ankle's swollen and ugly, too.
Its color now is reddish-blue.

The best things you can do for a sprain are:

1 Try not to use the injured part.
2 Elevate the injured part to help stop swelling.
3 A cold pack will help in the very beginning to
   ease the pain as well.
4 Take it easy for a few days.

One of the most easily damaged parts of your body is your skin.

I was feeling hungry and I had a hunch
that it was probably time to munch some lunch.
So I went into the kitchen all by myself,
to see what I could find upon the shelf.
I saw it in a moment, I didn't look far:
delicious peanut butter in a fine glass jar.
I took it down, opened it, and smelled it for a while.
Its wonderful aroma made my taste buds smile.
I took out a bagel (that's the kind of roll
that is round and tan with a center hole).
I was using a sharp knife to slice the bread,
when it accidentally slipped and cut my hand instead.

Kitchen

This way to the

The inside story

Taste bud

Cut

The cut bled a lot for a minute or so
But as I pressed, I slowed the flow.
Using soap and water, I washed it clean,
and making sure to follow the first-aid routine,
I put on a clean bandage just for protection,
to avoid the chance of getting an infection.*

The best things you can do when you get a cut are:

1 Wash it clean.
2 Place a clean cloth or a gauze pad over the wound and press down to stop the bleeding.
3 Put on a bandage, but make sure it's not too tight.
4 *Always* ask your mom, dad, or a grown-up for help. If the cut is serious, you should see a doctor.

*infection—when harmful germs enter the body and begin spreading

Infection

The Skin You're In & How It Mends

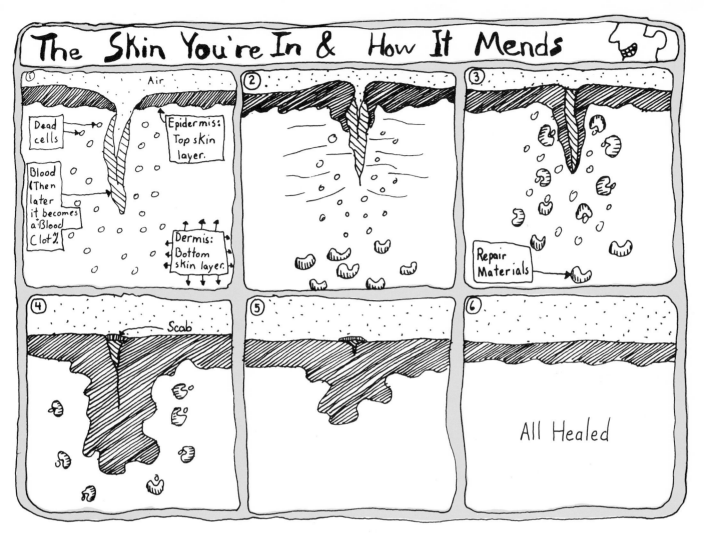

When your skin gets cut, it begins healing right away. Here's how:

1 Blood vessels are damaged and blood seeps into the wound, where it clots.
2 Fibers in the clot shrink and pull the wound's two edges together.
3 Cells on the cut's edges multiply and move into the clot, while dead cells are being moved out to clean the wound.
4 Blood brings in lots of repair materials, and new skin grows.
5 All of this happens under the scab, which is formed from the dried blood clot.
6 When enough time has passed and the skin is healed, the scab falls off.

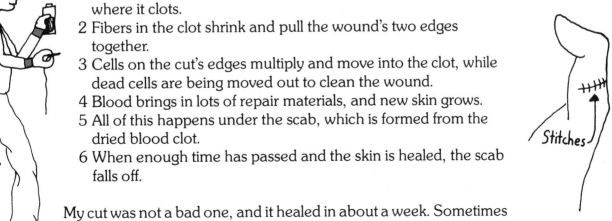

My cut was not a bad one, and it healed in about a week. Sometimes when the cut is extremely deep and/or wide, the doctor must use stitches to pull the cut's edges together.

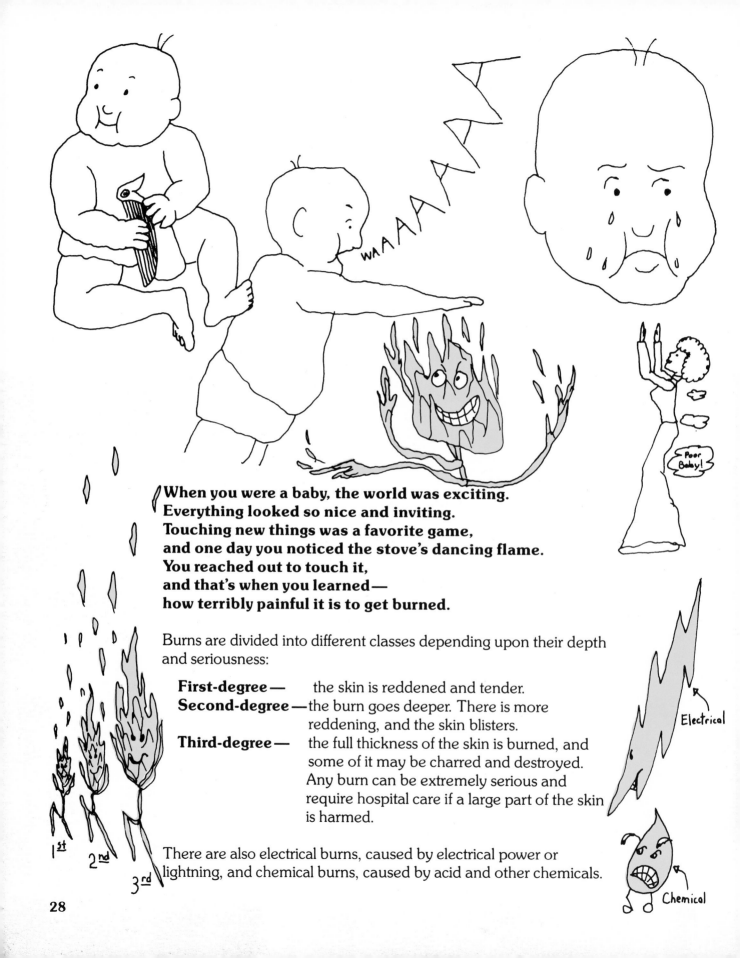

When you were a baby, the world was exciting.
Everything looked so nice and inviting.
Touching new things was a favorite game,
and one day you noticed the stove's dancing flame.
You reached out to touch it,
and that's when you learned—
how terribly painful it is to get burned.

Burns are divided into different classes depending upon their depth and seriousness:

First-degree — the skin is reddened and tender.
Second-degree — the burn goes deeper. There is more reddening, and the skin blisters.
Third-degree — the full thickness of the skin is burned, and some of it may be charred and destroyed. Any burn can be extremely serious and require hospital care if a large part of the skin is harmed.

There are also electrical burns, caused by electrical power or lightning, and chemical burns, caused by acid and other chemicals.

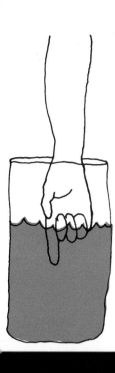

**You must take care where fire's concerned,
and be aware that you might get burned.
This lesson is important, so don't forget it.
For if you do, you're likely to regret it.**

With proper treatment, first- and second-degree burns can heal themselves. Here is some basic first-aid for burns:

1 Put injured area into cold water to relieve some of the pain.
2 Clean the area well.
3 Pat gently dry; don't rub.
4 Use a *non*-greasy burn ointment, the kind that can be rinsed off easily, to prevent infection of the damaged skin.

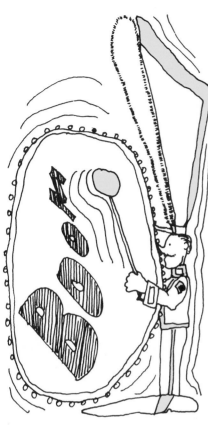

I can't seem to stop it.
It just keeps on coming.
A pounding that is sounding
like a soft but steady drumming.

The beating keeps repeating.
It's getting strong and loud.
It's not a solo drummer, no.
It feels more like a crowd.

I wish that I could stop it.
It's getting out of hand.
Now my head feels filled up
with a drummers' marching band.

The drummers form a circle
and go marching round my head.
There's really nothing I can do
but get into my bed.

There are lots of reasons people get headaches: because they are coming down with a cold; because they are tense or upset; or even because they are tired. If you get a headache that continues over a very long period of time, you should see a doctor. You might even want to have your vision checked.

**When you're feeling tense,
and a headache attacks,
it's just common sense
to try to relax.**

Sometimes aspirin helps relieve the pain, but since most headaches have a lot to do with emotions and the way you feel, you can probably do more for yourself by relaxing.

When you have a tension headache, it is a good idea to lie quietly in a darkened room, listen to soothing music, and just take it easy.

Aspirin

**When you're watching TV,
do you have to be
sitting real close to the screen?
Does it often occur
that the blackboard's a blur
'cause the words are too far to be seen?**

If the above is true for you, you may be *near-sighted.* This means you can see nearby things clearly, but you have trouble seeing things that are far away.

**When you read, must you place
your face in a space
quite far away from the book?
When things are too near,
are they blurred and unclear,
so you have to move back for a look?**

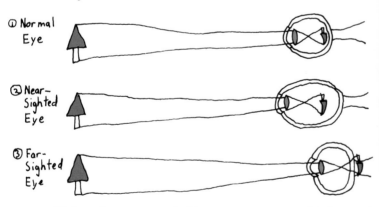

If the above sounds like you, you may be *far-sighted.* This means you can see faraway things clearly, but have trouble seeing things that are close up.

Another problem some people have with their vision is *color-blindness.* This means that they mix up colors like red and green.

If something is wrong with your sense of sight, your eyeballs are probably not shaped quite right. But don't let this problem give you a scare, glasses will help, if you wear the right pair.

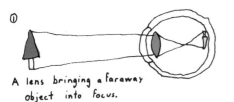

A lens bringing a faraway object into focus.

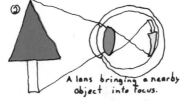

A lens bringing a nearby object into focus.

In order to see something, you need more than the object and your eyes. You need light. That's why you can't see in pitch blackness. When light falls on an object, some of it is reflected* and passes through your eye's cornea, pupil, and lens. The lens focuses the image** of the object on the retina.

If your eyeball is too long, the lens brings the image to a focus in front of the retina. This makes you near-sighted. If your eyeball is too short, the lens brings the image to a focus behind the retina. This makes you far-sighted.

Glasses bend the light rays so that a clear picture is formed on the retina. A special doctor called an *ophthalmologist* can check your eyes and find out what kind of glasses you need.

*reflected—light bounces off
**image—the object itself isn't in your eye, only its picture is. This picture is the image.

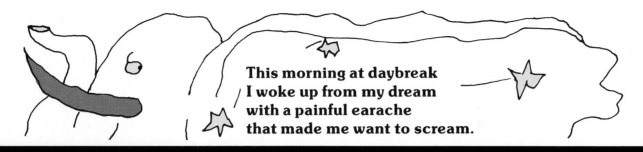
**This morning at daybreak
I woke up from my dream
with a painful earache
that made me want to scream.**

Earaches can be caused by lots of different things. An infection
building up, a small object from the outside getting caught inside,
an infection from the nose or throat that moves into the ear, or
sticking something pointed and sharp in your ear. Aside from being
so painful, earaches sometimes make it difficult to hear.

**Plop, plop, plop, plop,
in go the eardrops,
warm and soothing, helping to
relieve the pain I'm going through.**

Earaches can hurt an awful lot, so you'll want to take care of them as quickly as possible. Have your parents call a doctor who will help decide upon the best treatment for you.

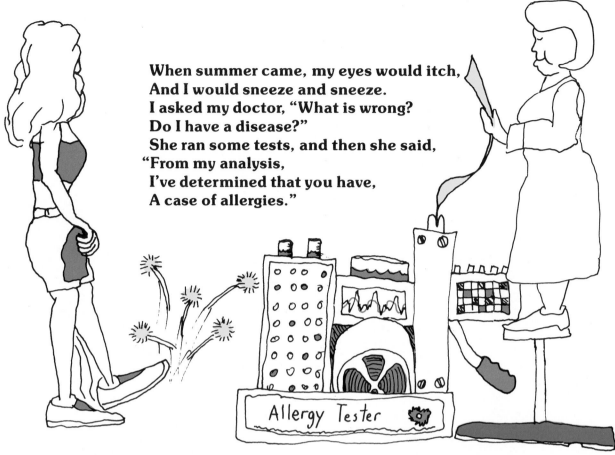

When summer came, my eyes would itch,
And I would sneeze and sneeze.
I asked my doctor, "What is wrong?
Do I have a disease?"
She ran some tests, and then she said,
"From my analysis,
I've determined that you have,
A case of allergies."

Allergy Tester

You have an allergy when some material that is harmless to most people causes an unusually bad reaction in your body, such as sneezing, itching, or skin bumps. You can be allergic to something you eat or drink, touch, breathe in the air or get as a medicine by mouth or injection.

Common allergies are:

1 **Hayfever**—caused by something that is carried in the air you breathe, such as dust, pollen, animal hair or dander, or feathers. Hayfever can cause sneezing, coughing, a runny nose, and itchy eyes.

2 **Asthma**—Most often caused by something you breathe in, including the viruses that cause colds.

3 **Hives**—usually caused by something you eat, especially foods like shellfish, strawberries, chocolate, eggs, or milk. You can also get hives from too much sunlight, insect bites, or medicine. Hives are very itchy red swellings (pimples or welts) that appear suddenly anywhere on the skin.

4 **Poison ivy and poison oak**—caused by touching certain plants. It gives some people a red itchy skin rash.

36

What can I do when I've got the aaaachooooz?
Go out and get a box of tissues.
Then play the detective and search for a clue
To discover what you are allergic to.
And another important thing on your list
Should be to go see the allergist.

Allergist

An allergist is a doctor specially trained to work with people who have allergies. He or she can do tests to find out exactly what's causing your allergy. In many cases you can take medicine or get allergy shots to help bring relief. Very often children outgrow their allergies.

The treatment for allergies depends on each individual case, but some general rules are:

1 Stay away from whatever's causing the trouble.
2 Keep in good shape with plenty of rest, exercise, and a good diet.
3 Relax when you are feeling tense.

Some people use wheelchairs to move them around.
Others use guide dogs to lead them through town.
Some people can't speak, while others can't hear,
and some people's thoughts are all vague and unclear.

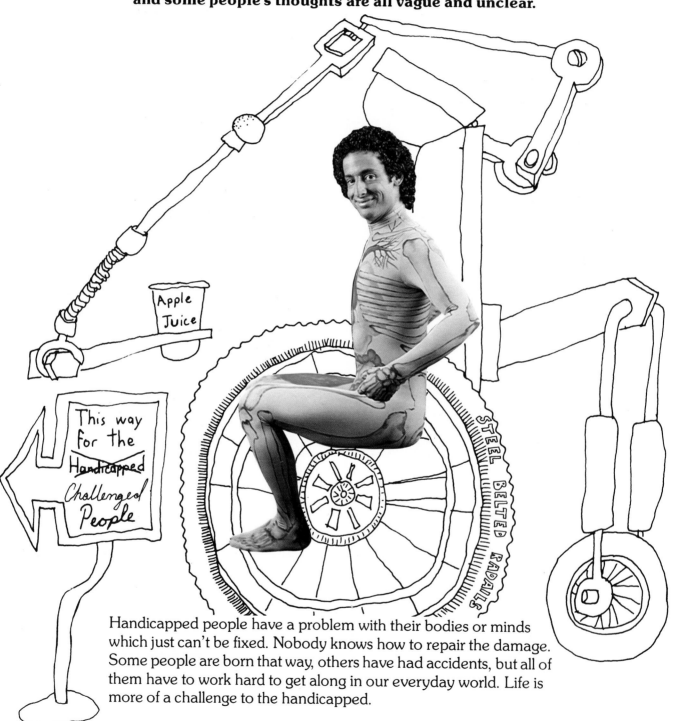

Apple Juice

This way for the ~~Handicapped~~ Challenged People

STEEL BELTED RADIALS

Handicapped people have a problem with their bodies or minds
which just can't be fixed. Nobody knows how to repair the damage.
Some people are born that way, others have had accidents, but all of
them have to work hard to get along in our everyday world. Life is
more of a challenge to the handicapped.

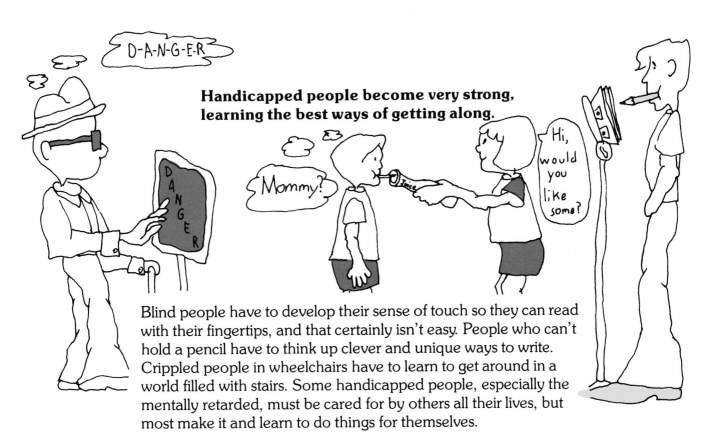

**Handicapped people become very strong,
learning the best ways of getting along.**

Blind people have to develop their sense of touch so they can read with their fingertips, and that certainly isn't easy. People who can't hold a pencil have to think up clever and unique ways to write. Crippled people in wheelchairs have to learn to get around in a world filled with stairs. Some handicapped people, especially the mentally retarded, must be cared for by others all their lives, but most make it and learn to do things for themselves.

Sometimes it seems a little bit scary being with somebody who is blind, crippled, or handicapped in some other way. You may not know what to do. You might feel a little funny because you want to stare. Well, go ahead...

**Stop, stare,
question if you dare.**

Get to know the person and you will see that he or she is as much a person as you are. It may take awhile, but it will be worth it.

The dentist said, "Open up wide,
I want to take a look inside.
Um-hum, ah-ha, what's this I see?
It seems you've got a cavity."

Cavity

X-RAY

Small pieces of food stay in your mouth after you eat. If you don't clean them out, they can help cause cavities. Here's how:

1 There is a sticky film called *plaque* which is always forming on your teeth. It is made from the bacteria that live in your mouth.
2 Some of the food you eat gets stuck on and between your teeth and gums.
3 Some of the bacteria in the plaque change the sugars and starches into acid.
4 This acid begins to eat away at the enamel* on your tooth, creating a cavity.

Since most "junk foods" have a lot of sugar, they can be changed into a lot of acid, which can mean a lot of cavities.

*enamel—the smooth hard outer layer of the tooth

1. Plaque

2. Sticky Food

3. Acid

4. Cavities

40

**Brush in the morning, again at night,
and floss every single day.
That will keep your teeth clean and white,
and help prevent decay.**

Teeth's Best Friends

Dental Floss

Celery

If you do get a cavity, the dentist will remove the decayed part and seal it with a filling.

A lot of cavities can be prevented by cutting down on sweets, eating healthy foods, and, most important, brushing and flossing every day (if possible, after every meal).

Remember, flossing is just as important as brushing. With floss you can get into the tight places where food gets stuck and can't be reached with brush bristles.

Visit your dentist twice a year. She or he will be happy to work with you and teach you the correct way to clean your teeth and care for your gums.

You can help keep your teeth clean by eating a piece of raw vegetable or fruit, such as celery, carrot, or apple, after the meal.

Toothbrush

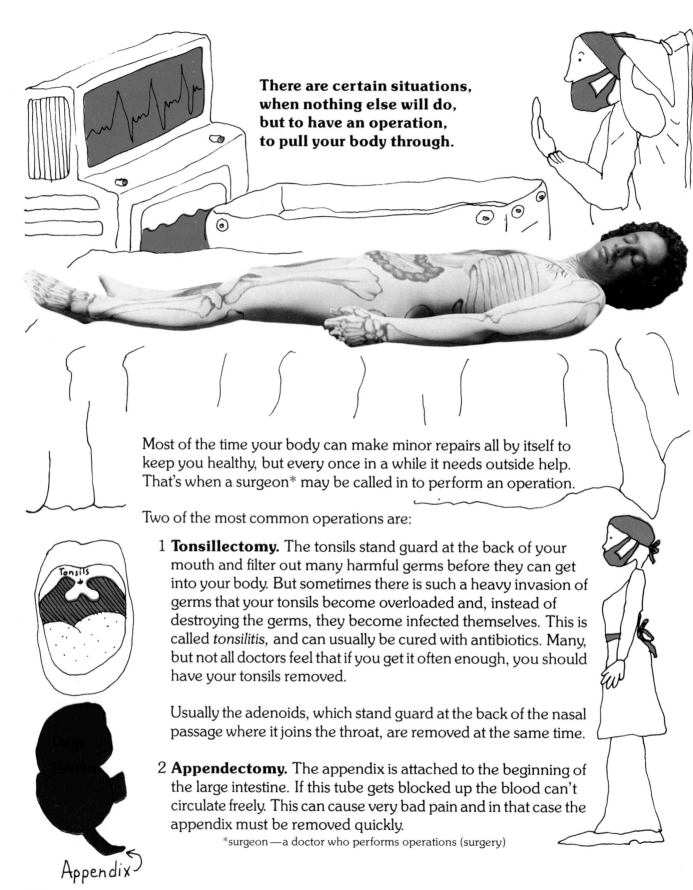

**There are certain situations,
when nothing else will do,
but to have an operation,
to pull your body through.**

Most of the time your body can make minor repairs all by itself to keep you healthy, but every once in a while it needs outside help. That's when a surgeon* may be called in to perform an operation.

Two of the most common operations are:

1 **Tonsillectomy.** The tonsils stand guard at the back of your mouth and filter out many harmful germs before they can get into your body. But sometimes there is such a heavy invasion of germs that your tonsils become overloaded and, instead of destroying the germs, they become infected themselves. This is called *tonsilitis,* and can usually be cured with antibiotics. Many, but not all doctors feel that if you get it often enough, you should have your tonsils removed.

Usually the adenoids, which stand guard at the back of the nasal passage where it joins the throat, are removed at the same time.

2 **Appendectomy.** The appendix is attached to the beginning of the large intestine. If this tube gets blocked up the blood can't circulate freely. This can cause very bad pain and in that case the appendix must be removed quickly.

*surgeon—a doctor who performs operations (surgery)

Tonsils

Large Intestine

Appendix

42

When I got sick, I had to dwell
in a building with beds and a funny smell.
I learned something there I'd like to tell —
a hospital is really a GET-WELL HOTEL.

Quiet Please

Get-Well Hotel

Push for Light

If you have to go into a hospital, remember, it's sometimes the best place to be for the extra-special care you may need to get well soon.

Aside from operations, people go into hospitals to rest, for tests and X-rays, and to learn new ways of keeping healthy. Hospitals also train doctors and nurses to recognize and treat diseases.

**There is really so much I can mention
about your body and mine,
to bring facts to your attention
about sickness and feeling fine.**

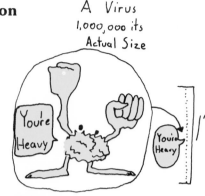

1 About 90 percent of all Americans get at least one cold every year, and 50 percent get more than one.

2 Viruses are so small that if you lined them up it would take from 83,000 to 1,555,000 to make an inch.

3 There are at least thirty known kinds of cold viruses.

4 Flu is most common during the winter months.

5 Your body temperature changes throughout the day. It is lowest in the early morning and highest in the late afternoon.

6 Chicken pox is one of the most contagious of all human diseases.

7 Falls and automobile accidents are responsible for more broken bones than any other kinds of accidents.

8 The most common fracture is a tipped-back break of the forearm, called a *Colles fracture*. You're most likely to get it trying to stop a fall with outstretched hands.

9 Often the healing of a fracture is so complete that eventually you can't detect it even with X-rays.

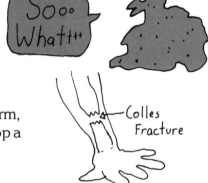

10 Skin heals so incredibly well that when a severely injured fingertip heals, even the fingerprint whorls return to their regular pattern.

11 It is believed that almost every adult has had a headache at one time or another.

12 About one out of every ten people is allergic to something.

13 There are special glasses which help correct vision but can't be seen. They're called contact lenses.

14 Tooth decay is the most common problem of school-aged children.

15 Almost half the area of your teeth can't be reached with a toothbrush. Dental floss is used to get those hard-to-clean spots.

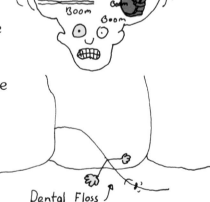

16 Sugarless gum is not really sugarless, but the natural sweeteners are not harmful to your teeth.

17 The first recorded use of an antibiotic was over 2,500 years ago in China.

18 Almost one in seven people goes into the hospital for one reason or another every year.

19 Your body can repair itself quickly. Blood cells are replaced within hours, skin within days, and bones within weeks.

I didn't have a place
for lots of information,
so I've made a special space
for extra explanations.

1 Why do you blow your nose when you get sick?

When a virus moves in, your body protects itself by producing a lot of mucus. When you blow your nose, you are washing many germs out of your body.

2 What is pneumonia?

Pneumonia is a very severe infection of the lungs. It brings high fever, a cough, and sometimes sharp chest pains. Some pneumonia is caused by bacteria, some by viruses.

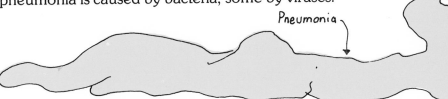

Pneumonia

3 What are swollen glands?

Glands are parts of your body that have many jobs to do. One of the most important is to act as a filter to prevent infection from entering your bloodstream. If one gets swollen or especially tender in your neck, this tells you there is most probably an infection in your head area.

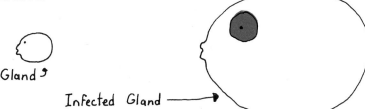

Gland

Infected Gland

4 What causes a black-and-blue mark?

When you get a bruise, some of the small blood vessels under the skin get broken. Blood collects in the area, causing swelling and discoloration (black and blue).

5 What are sinuses?

Sinuses are spaces within the skull, or air spaces in the skull bones.

Sinuses ⟶

6 What is a muscle strain?

A muscle strain is an overstretching or tearing of a muscle or its tendon. A tendon connects the muscle to the bone. Strains are usually caused by lifting something heavy when you are not in a good position to do it.

7 What causes diarrhea?

Diarrhea is a very loose bowel movement which may occur anywhere from three to twenty times a day. It can be caused by tension, infection, or something you ate.

Hot
Chili

8 What are scalds?

Scalds are skin burns caused by boiling water or steam.

9 What is frostbite?

With frostbite, the skin of the nose, ears, fingers, or toes becomes so cold that blood can't circulate freely. At first there is reddening, then swelling, then blistering, and finally the skin can die. Frostbite is very similar to burns, but it is caused by cold, not heat.

10 What are antibodies?

Antibodies are part of your body's defense system. When there is a germ invader, special cells in your body produce certain chemical substances that weaken or destroy it. These chemical defenders are called antibodies.

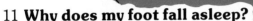

11 Why does my foot fall asleep?

It all begins with nerves. Nerves are special cells which carry messages from your brain to all the different parts of your body, and back again. When you sit in some positions for too long the main nerve in your leg gets squeezed and stops sending information to your brain. When this happens you no longer feel your foot and it seems like it's asleep. Moving around takes the pressure off the nerve and wakes your foot up.

12 What is inflammation?

When there is an injury to your body caused by bacteria, viruses, heat, cold, etc., blood quickly flows to the area, causing it to get red and hot. As the blood brings materials to repair the damage, there is swelling. This redness, swelling, and heat are called *inflammation*.

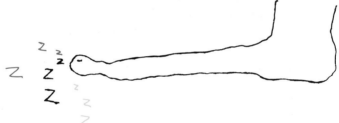

13 What is fluoride?

Fluoride is a chemical that is added to drinking water or put directly on your teeth by your dentist. It helps prevent tooth decay.

**Your parents can help,
doctors can, too,
but a healthy life
is up to you!**

Remember, your body belongs to you. It's got a tremendous power
to heal itself, but it needs your help. Getting to know it, eating well,
exercising, and resting are all necessary, but I think the most
important thing you can do for your health can be explained in two
words:

LOVE YOURSELF